US MILITARY FORCES

NAVY

By Jeanne Nagle

Gareth Stevens
Publishing

Please visit our website, www.garethstevens.com. For a free color catalog of all our high-quality books, call toll free 1-800-542-2595 or fax 1-877-542-2596.

Library of Congress Cataloging-in-Publication Data

Nagle, Jeanne.
Navy / Jeanne Nagle.
    p. cm. — (US military forces)
Includes index.
ISBN 978-1-4339-5860-1 (pbk.)
ISBN 978-1-4339-5861-8 (6-pack)
ISBN 978-1-4339-5858-8 (library binding)
1. United States. Navy—Juvenile literature. 2. United States. Navy—History—Juvenile literature. 3. United States—History, Naval—Juvenile literature. I. Title.
VA58.4.N34 2012
359.00973—dc22

2011009416

First Edition

Published in 2012 by
Gareth Stevens Publishing
111 East 14th Street, Suite 349
New York, NY 10003

Copyright © 2012 Gareth Stevens Publishing

Designer: Michael J. Flynn
Editor: Greg Roza

Photo credits: Cover, p. 1 Stocktrek Images/the Agency Collection/Getty Images; pp. 5 (all), 19 (USS *Constitution*) Shutterstock.com; pp. 6–7 MPI/Archive Photos/Getty Images; p. 8 Buyenlarge/Archive Photos/Getty Images; p. 9 Central Press/Archive Photos/Getty Images; p. 10 Chip Somodevilla/Getty Images; pp. 11 (all), 26 Hulton Archive/Getty Images; p. 12 Joe Raedle/Getty Images; pp. 13, 17 Stocktrek/Getty Images; p. 15 Scott Nelson/Getty Images; p. 16 Kim Jae-Hwan/AFP/Getty Images; pp. 18–19, 20, 21 U.S. Navy/Getty Images; p. 23 Joel Sartore/National Geographic/Getty Images; p. 24 Stock Montage/Archive Photos/Getty Images; p. 25 Frank Turgent/Archive Photos/Getty Images; p. 27 Time & Life Pictures/Getty Images; pp. 28–29 Business Wire/Getty Images.

Printed in the United States of America

CPSIA compliance information: Batch #CS11GS: For further information contact Gareth Stevens, New York, New York at 1-800-542-2595.

CONTENTS

Words in the glossary appear in **bold** type the first time they are used in the text.

WHAT IS THE NAVY?

The navy is the US military branch that guards the seas. When the United States is at war, the navy battles enemy ships and fires on land targets from the sea. Navy ships also move troops to and from different battlegrounds. Navy pilots attack from the air. Warplanes and helicopters land on huge navy ships called aircraft carriers.

During peacetime, the navy's main job is making sure US citizens can sail the world's oceans safely. In fact, some people think navy ships actually help keep the peace simply by sailing around the world and showing possible enemies US might.

The Naval Academy

The United States Naval Academy, which trains men and women to be navy officers, was founded in 1845. Located in Annapolis, Maryland, the Naval Academy teaches the same kinds of courses as regular colleges. Students called cadets also learn about navy history and military life.

The Navy destroyer USS *Laboon* takes part in the Parade of Sails on the Elizabeth River in Norfolk, Virginia.

IMPORTANT MOMENTS IN NAVY HISTORY

In 1775, two armed American ships were sent to **intercept** guns and supplies being sent to British troops in the American colonies. More ships were soon added to what became known as the Continental navy, which fought the British during the American Revolution. The US Department of the Navy, which is the official government navy office, was formed in 1798.

The Continental navy, led by John Paul Jones, defeated the British navy during a battle on September 22, 1779.

During the American Civil War (1861–1865), the navy added iron plating to its ships. These sheets of metal acted like armor to protect the wood underneath. Today, it's common for navy ships to be made of steel.

The Navy Song

The song "Anchors Aweigh" was originally written as a march for a class of Naval Academy cadets. Today, it's played as a fight song at academy sporting events. The tune is also considered the navy's unofficial **anthem**.

During the Spanish-American War (1898), the navy won many victories over the Spanish **Armada**, one of the best navies in the world. After that, the United States was known as a naval superpower.

On December 7, 1941, Japanese fliers staged a surprise attack on navy ships at Pearl Harbor in the Hawaiian Islands. The attack drove the United States to enter World War II.

The navy has fought in several wars and conflicts since World War II, including those in Vietnam, Iraq, and Afghanistan. Today's navy is made up of more than 325,000 active-duty members, with nearly 300 ships (including submarines) and more than 3,700 aircraft.

During the Battle of Santiago de Cuba, the US Navy destroyed the Spanish fleet stationed in the Caribbean.

The USS *Missouri* fires on enemies in North Korea during the Korean War in 1951.

Surprise Attack

The attack on Pearl Harbor lasted 2 hours. Eighteen ships and 350 navy planes were damaged or destroyed. More important, 3,500 Americans on the base were killed or wounded. Almost half of those were sailors on one ship, the USS *Arizona*.

LINE OF COMMAND

The secretary of the navy is the head of the US Department of the Navy. This official oversees recruiting (getting people to join the navy), making sure ships and bases have supplies, and sending troops off to battle. The person in charge of active-duty sailors is the chief of naval operations. Each official has many assistants working under them.

As a group, active-duty sailors are called the operating forces. Sailors are either **enlisted** or **commissioned**. Enlisted sailors, called recruits, join without any special training. Commissioned sailors have attended the Naval Academy or some other kind of officer-training program.

On May 28, 2010, the US Naval Academy held its 106th graduation ceremony.

Franklin D. Roosevelt

Naval Presidents

Two US presidents held the same important position within the Department of the Navy before being elected to lead the country. Theodore Roosevelt was appointed assistant secretary of the navy in 1897. Sixteen years later, his cousin, Franklin Delano Roosevelt, was named to the same post.

Theodore Roosevelt

NAVY JOBS

There are many jobs for sailors on naval vessels. Ship workers include **navigators**, who help guide or steer ships. **Technicians** operate and take care of equipment for communications, tracking, and other tasks.

On battleships, gunner's mates keep weapons in working order and fire them during battle. On aircraft carriers, there are sailors who help land planes and mechanics who fix and keep aircraft in good condition. Navy airmen are pilots who fly the aircraft. During battle, they bomb targets and fire guns. Navy pilots also perform reconnaissance. This means they fly over areas and report what they see.

These men are navy shooters. They work on aircraft carriers and help planes take off safely.

A gunner's mate fires a machine gun during training aboard the USS *Boxer*.

Bells on Board

On board a ship, time is broken into 4-hour periods known as watches. Bells ring eight times during each watch to tell what time it is. Bells are also rung on navy ships to let the crew know there's an important person on board.

Sailors in the navy mostly work in one of two main areas. The operating forces are made up of nine groups spread out all over the globe. Each group is designed to prepare naval forces for military combat.

Jobs such as training sailors, building and repairing ships, and naval **intelligence** are handled by the shore establishment. The people who work these jobs are a combination of sailors and **civilians**. They work on naval bases located in US cities on the East and the West Coasts and on bases around the world. Some work on naval ships, too.

Modern-Day Pirates

In the 21st century, the navy has had to fight an enemy it hasn't fought in a long time—pirates. Navy ships have shot at and captured several modern-day pirates off the coasts of Africa and the Middle East.

A crewman on the USS *Constellation* works on an F/A-18 Hornet.

SPECIAL FORCES

Formed in 1962, the navy SEALs are a special unit that performs very risky missions. The unit's name shows where it fights—on the **SE**a, in the **A**ir, and on **L**and.

What Are Seabees?

The Seabees may be considered the construction crew of the navy. They build roads, landing strips, and bases in war-torn areas. Their work helps the operating forces do their jobs more easily. The Seabee saying is "We Build, We Fight."

Navy SEALs are trained in **guerrilla** fighting. They go on secret missions meant to weaken the enemy's ability to fight. To do this, they must get close to enemy forces. They also make sure battle zones are clear of land mines and enemy fighters.

Special training for navy SEALs includes scuba diving, jumping from helicopters into the water, and parachuting out of planes. SEALs also learn about explosives.

This navy SEAL is using an oxygen rebreather instead of a regular oxygen tank. A rebreather recycles the air a diver breathes out.

TYPES OF NAVY SHIPS

Navy ships come in different sizes and speeds. There are seven types of vessels: aircraft carriers, **amphibious** assault ships, battleships, cruisers, destroyers, frigates, and submarines.

The USS *Dwight D. Eisenhower* aircraft carrier can carry up to 90 planes and helicopters.

USS Constitution

The first ship ever put into service by the navy was the USS *Constitution*. Paul Revere made the bolts that hold the wooden frigate together. British forces nicknamed the ship "Old Ironsides" because shots bounced off her metal-plated hull. The *Constitution* is docked in Boston Harbor.

The name "aircraft carrier" describes this class of ship perfectly. Inside are **hangars** where warplanes are carried. Huge elevators lift planes up to long flight decks, where they take off and land. **Catapults** help planes reach take-off speed quickly, while hooks and cables bring landing planes to a swift stop. Aircraft carriers are so big they're considered US territory—like states on the water.

Amphibious ships work in the water and on land. These ships move troops, vehicles, weapons, and supplies from deep water right up onto beaches and shores. The largest of these vessels, called amphibious assault ships, even carry smaller amphibious ships. Some also have room for helicopters to land on their decks.

Cruisers are medium-size ships that are heavily armed. Weapons on board a cruiser include guns, guided missiles, and **torpedoes**. Cruisers can hit several targets at once. These targets can be on land, at sea, in the air, or underwater.

Battleships

The first battleship went into service in 1895. These large, heavily armed ships were important fighting vessels for years, especially during both World Wars. Hard to move and expensive to operate, battleships were replaced by cruisers and destroyers. By 1992, battleships were no longer part of the active navy.

A Tomahawk missile is launched from the cruiser USS *Cape St. George*.

Destroyers move faster than cruisers. They're designed to defend other navy ships against torpedo boats, which are small and very quick. Destroyers are equipped with guns on their decks and torpedo tubes down below.

The first job of frigates is to protect and refuel other ships during battles. But these warships are also able to fight submarines. Most ships of the Continental navy were frigates.

The navy also has two types of submarines—attack and ballistic. Ballistic submarines fire **nuclear** missiles instead of torpedoes. The largest submarines can carry about 150 sailors at a time.

Ship Names

The secretary of the navy is in charge of naming new ships, but many others contribute. A list of possible names is gathered from research into navy history and the suggestions of active-duty sailors, retired sailors, and even the general public.

Los Angeles–class attack submarines, like the one shown here, can launch missiles at land targets while underwater.

FAMOUS NAVAL FIGURES

Many people have become famous for their service in the US Navy. As a lieutenant in the Continental navy, John Paul Jones was honored for capturing and destroying several British ships during the American Revolution. When asked if he would surrender during a fierce battle, John Paul Jones famously answered by saying, "I have not yet begun to fight!"

John Paul Jones

Admiral David Farragut was admired for many Union victories during the American Civil War. Another commander, Matthew C. Perry, was famous for noncombat actions. He sailed a few ships to Japan in the 1850s and convinced the Japanese to open trade and **diplomatic** relations with the United States.

President Kennedy: Navy Hero

Before he was president, John F. Kennedy was a war hero. During World War II, Kennedy was captain of a patrol boat that sank in 1943. He rescued many wounded crew members. Kennedy supposedly pulled one sailor to safety by swimming with the strap of the man's life vest in his teeth.

When she enlisted in the navy **reserve** in 1917, during World War I, Loretta Perfectus Walsh became the first woman to serve in any branch of the US military as something other than a nurse. In 1942, Mildred McAfee became the navy's first female commissioned officer.

McAfee also served as the first director of Women Accepted for Volunteer Emergency Service (WAVES). This all-female division was formed during World War II. Many thought women would be in the navy only as long as the "emergency"—the war—lasted. It turned out that the WAVES opened the door for women to have navy careers.

Don't miss your great opportunity..

THE NAVY NEEDS YOU IN THE **WAVES**

The Yeomen (F) were sometimes called "Yeomanettes" or "Yeowomen."

Yeomen (F)

During World War I, the navy had an all-women enlisted division known as Yeomen (F). The "F" stood for "female." Most of these women were secretaries and office workers. Many of them concluded their navy service when the war ended.

THE FUTURE OF THE US NAVY

The navy is preparing for the future through new technology. Smaller, faster warships are being built that can move more easily in different directions. Also, more "smart ships," which are operated mainly by computer, are being added to the fleet. The navy is also experimenting with advanced weapons such as a radar-guided laser beam that can destroy enemy planes.

Working closely with other military branches is also in the navy's future. The AirSea Battle Concept calls for the air force and the navy to work together to locate and defeat enemy forces. One thing that won't change is the navy's dedication to protecting the United States and its citizens.

Navy Green

The official navy colors are blue and gold, but soon green may be added to that. The secretary of the navy announced in 2010 that the navy should use energy sources that create less pollution. Using **biofuel** instead of oil and gas is one goal for the navy.

An unmanned aircraft takes off from the deck of an aircraft carrier.

GLOSSARY

amphibious: having the capability to operate on both land and water

anthem: a song declaring loyalty to a group, cause, or country

armada: a large fleet of warships

biofuel: a fuel made from plants that doesn't cause as much pollution as other fuels

catapult: a machine for getting an airplane into the air at flying speed very quickly

civilian: a person not on active duty in the military

commissioned: referring to people in the military who are made officers and given special rank

diplomatic: having to do with official relations between countries

enlisted: members of the military who rank below commissioned officers

guerrilla: having to do with irregular or secretive military methods

hangar: an enclosed area where planes are kept and repaired

intelligence: the gathering of secret information about enemies

intercept: to stop or interrupt the delivery of something

navigator: the person who maps out a course of travel

nuclear: having to do with the enormous power created by splitting atoms, the smallest bits of matter

reserve: referring to soldiers who are not part of a country's main forces, but may be called to active duty in times of need

technician: a person who has special training in using equipment

torpedo: a missile that travels underwater

Books

Adamson, Thomas K. *U.S. Navy Submarines*. Mankato, MN: Capstone Press, 2006.

David, Jack. *United States Navy*. Minneapolis, MN: Bellwether Media, 2008.

Yomtov, Nelson. *Navy SEALs in Action*. New York, NY: Bearport Publishing, 2008.

Websites

Military Kidz Installation
www.militarykidz.com
After creating their own special ID card, kids can learn about military communications, attend boot camp, or play games.

Tour of USS PAMPANITO
www.maritime.org/tour/index.php
Take a virtual tour of a navy submarine, now docked in San Francisco, California, and learn about its adventures during World War II.

INDEX